FADE TO BLACK

Thoughts on Black Americans

*To Bennie
thanks for your
support and help.
your classmate
Woody Campbell*

Woody Campbell

BOOKS WITH PASSION

Houston, Texas

2007

Copyright © 2007 Woody Campbell

Against the Wind
An Imprint of Bluebonnets Boots & Books Press
11010 Hanning Lane
Houston, TX 77041-5006
713-896-9887 fax

www.FadeToBlack-TheBook.com

Campbell, Woody.
    Fade to black : thoughts on Black Americans / Woody
        Campbell.
    p. cm.
    Includes bibliographical references.
    ISBN 978-09645493-9-5 (hardback)
    ISBN 978-09645493-5-7 (perfect)
    ISBN 978-09645493-8-8 (ebook)
1. African Americans—Race identity. 2. United States—Race
    relations. 3. Self-perception. 4. Group identity. I. Title.
E185.625 .C35 2007   155.849—dc22

Production Team
Rita Mills of The Book Connection — Project Manager
Peggy Stautberg & Anita Bunkley — Editing Team
Line Editing — Faye Walker

Gladys Ramirez — Cover Design

The paper used in this publication meets the requirements of the American National Standard for Permanence of Paper for Printed Library Materials Z39.48-1984.

Printed in the United States of America

Table of Contents

Dedication

Ms. Verdell (Aunt Honey, Handful? Momma): You are gone now and we can no longer hear your laughter, enjoy your wit or listen to the good stories of the old days about our grandparents or relatives. Nor can we hear your intellect and thoughtful guidance, the confident tutoring of your knowledge that extended far beyond the years of an education unjustly denied.

Although we can no longer take your hand and tell you how much we care, you are still with us. You are in our thoughts each time we remember family or loved ones. You are part of each response to a familiar or unknown situation using the knowledge you taught us from the days of our youth. You are with us in our children, each of whom you touched in your own unique way, so that you are endeared in their hearts and memories.

We see you in the talents you passed along to each of us. Those little pieces of you that we each carry allow you to live on far beyond your mortal days. In James you have left your fun-loving personality and the hard work ethic etched in the features of the Johnson you were born. Ernestine carries your basic goodness and the refusal to see the unkind character of any person. In Ora, there is the fiery temper but intense fidelity to the maternal instinct, which bears the family matriarchal tradition. In me, there is your quiet, intuitive wisdom and the ability to see within and understand people.

Through God's wisdom you were loaned to us to enrich our lives with your presence, your influence, and to teach us to reach beyond our humble origins to become the people that he intended. He (God) gave you the humanity that would never allow you to turn away a wounded thing or a person in need, regardless of their station or lot in life. That trait endeared you to all who knew and loved you. Whether it was by giving of yourself, your presence or whatever you had, you always left people better for having known you, even if it meant often getting less in return.

We were blessed to have known you. We were more blessed to have shared you for much of your four-score and two years of life. Thanks to you, each day as we grow, each triumph we may claim, whatever imprint we may leave as part of our legacy, we owe to you and to God for sending you.

You belong now to the ages and to God, who chose to reclaim you. Your work has been done and you can now rest with the angels. You will forever be in our hearts and we will endeavor to gain strength from that and to pass along what you have shared with us. We were honored to have known you, enriched that you shared your life with us and blessed that God sent you to be Our Mom. Rest in peace, O Gentle Spirit!

—wlc

Preface

For many years, I have been very troubled by the apparent fact that we as Black Americans of African descent—whose ancestors had not immigrated willingly to America—have been unable to settle on a definitive identity. Who are we? Who decided that we were African Americans? How did the world conclude that to be our designation? As children growing up, we were called, with apparent acceptance, "Colored people." By the time the Civil Rights movement was ushered in by Dr. Martin Luther King, Jr., we were elevated to the respectable status of "Negro." In college, I saw us move to "Afro American" and then to the preferred "Black American," which I thought represented the result of the efforts of slain martyrs like Medgar Evers and Dr. Martin Luther King, Jr., who perished so that we could be known as Black Americans. They died so that we could move forward and share in the fruits of our labor in America.

In the years following the death of Dr. King,

we drifted into and out of various Afro-centric manifestations of dress and ties to continental Africa that eventually led us hesitantly to become African Americans. I use the term "hesitantly" because it came about gradually and not with full conviction by overwhelming acceptance. I have never really seen the conviction in it or an understanding of what it means. I have seen enough disagreement with that position (including my own) that I finally wanted to take a thoughtful look at our identity crisis and try to find some logical foundation for who we are and how it came to be. In so doing, I did not want to create another Black history book or a book about slavery although it is clear that the two are integrally related to the problem. I also want to stay away from a regurgitation of a list of statistics that can often be used as self-serving proof sources. I simply wanted to use thought and logic, combined with known facts and realities, to arrive at an acceptable conclusion-a conclusion that is the result of a cognitive process rather than some popular wave that is without thought, reason or analysis.

I am unable to understand why this has not been done before. I feel that there are thousands, if not millions, of people who feel as I do but for some reason, perhaps the fear of expert opinion, have not demonstrated their opposition. For all of those people, let me state without hesitation that I believe we are

Black Americans of African descent. The African American designation is by definition and logic a mis-representation.

FADE TO BLACK

CHAPTER 1

The Issue for Black Americans

There is no subject of greater urgency to me than the Black Americans' long and continued search for identity. It is centuries old and still present. We are a volatile, confused lot. Confused because, unlike most other people in America, we have never really come to grips with our past, with who we are! The late Black author James Baldwin believed that to go anywhere you first had to know where you are from. I believe that this simple principle-or more precisely, the lack of it, is one of the root causes of what plagues Black Americans. We have never really acceptably answered the question of who we are. Are we Africans, Niggers, Negroes, Colored People, Afro Americans, Black Americans, or today's accepted version, African Americans?

Having lived through a lot of these name changes, and frankly, being perplexed by the frequency of change, I have come to a conclusion that I firmly support and believe this writing provides a starting point to what I hope will be a sound, believable position.

I do not want this writing to degenerate into another Black history book or become so laden with statistics or fancy concepts, psychological or otherwise, that my message is buried somewhere between statistics and intellectual rhetoric. At the same time, I realize that to go where I hope to go with this written account, I cannot escape considering and writing about Black history.

I believe that I am an American, a Black American to be specific. I am a product of and a part of the fabric of America. To be sure, I am a Black American of African descent, but from there the picture gets a little gray.

I would like to take a page from Descartes, the early French philosopher who chose to "think" to prove his existence. His rationale was: "I think, therefore I am." I am going to simply take a thinking, rational approach to who I and Black Americans in general are. You will notice that I did not say "Black people" but Black Americans because there is a difference.

The reason I want to emphasize thinking and practicality is very simply that there was a time when it was okay, in fact laudable, to think. Today, we are so accustomed to being told what and how to think that it is something of a lost art. The act of independent thought is subjected to the "curse" of enlightenment, which is expert opinion and analysis. This has become such an intimidation that it has had the affect of limiting thought. As a result, people are more easily silenced and herded to whatever persuasion is desired by the sources wielding the power.

I have often thought that if I had to write a book about the American Black experience I would title it *Slavery—The Birth of a People* because it sums up the progression that the African slaves went through to become the Black Americans that we are. Since our ancestry was undoubtedly African, it is also very understandable that the description "African" would be a part of our racial designation or identity. However, from the time that slavery was introduced into the colonies to the time that the slaves were freed by the Emancipation Proclamation and the Civil War, the "original" African virtually disappeared and in his place, the harsh reality of two and one half centuries of slavery left an even heartier race of people of color: the American Negro. Although he retained the dark skin and some of the recognizable features characteristic of his African ancestry, the cruel and dehumanizing experience of slavery spawned a very different people of color whose kinship can be linked by only one certainty, slavery! Therefore, to understand who we are, it stands to reason that as Black Americans, we must begin with slavery.

That in itself is a problem for many black people. Slavery was devastating to the American Negro. It destroyed many people, scattered families and left a stigma of shame on Black people, especially in America, that many have not been able to accept. As a result, we can see over the years a pattern in the Black American's search for identity, a popular trend to bypass the experience of slavery in our search for identity. A manifestation of this has been the adoption of African dress and cultural customs. Another example is the popularity of various Black Muslim sects and the adoption of Muslim names and the Islamic religion. The problem that this presents is that it is just as, if not more, confusing to the central question of who we are.

When I try to match the people that we are as Black Americans to the countries and people that we claim to be, I see even more contradiction and confusion. These contradictions are both cultural and individual. I am more at odds with the cultures we claim than I am with the stigma of slavery that I seek to avoid. What is it that makes me so different from the African brother that I stand next to? Our cultural contrasts visually jump out so strongly that if you placed me next to a Caucasian American, the differences, except for skin tone, are less obvious.

The fact that we live in a society that promotes misconceptions, particularly if there is money to be made, has not helped Black Americans establish and hold to an identity. Add to that the tendency to follow what is popular regardless of how unsound, and you have an environment that promotes a mindset that swings like a pendulum. The absence of a strong polarizing force like a Dr. Martin Luther King, Jr. has been a factor in allowing the pendulum to swing as freely as it has. Today, Black Americans are collectively and individually referred to as African Americans. I have always had difficulty with that, and I am sure there are others who feel the same. For all of us Black Americans who feel that way, I hope that this establishes once and for all who we are and why we feel that way. I, for one, have had enough of the confusion. I am not mixed up about who I am! Five years from now, when someone comes along with another name or description to decide what I am, let it be known that this is where I get off! I am a Black American! Of African descent yes, but a Black American!

There are certain attributes or characteristics that cause a group of people to be recognized as a race of people.

- A common language—Some races are tribal, however, and do speak different languages
- Genetic similarity

- Social order and traditions that define a culture
- The family unit as a central and stabilizing factor
- The ability to pass on heritage and culture

The Africans had all these characteristics in their homeland. However, when they emerged thousands of miles and months removed from that reality as slaves in America, they were destined to centuries of hardships that afforded them little chance to function as a race of people. They were captives in a hostile land thousands of miles from what was familiar to them with little or no chance to reclaim their lives or to continue their cultures as they knew them.

Slavery was absolute in its authority and was granted more power by the recognition of the Fugitive Slave Laws enacted by some states that recognized slaves not as people but as property. Some will argue that not all slave owners were harsh, that some were benevolent and treated their slaves well. My response to that is that if they were truly benevolent they would not have had slaves. Recognized as property and treated as such, the African slave did not have the freedom and rights to function as a race of people. They lived in and under a system of total subjugation and servitude. They were property. This ultimately had a profound affect on those attributes that are common to a race of people. The African slave was transformed into the American Negro, leaving behind most of his African past and taking on a new identity. The transformation was gradual, but there was a definite metamorphosis. As we look at the impact of the change on the African slaves that entered the borders of the United States, let us keep in mind the contrast of the native African (and the intensely tribal nature of that existence) and the fact that it existed virtually unchanged, in contrast to the subjugated existence of the Black African slave in America.

CHAPTER 2

A Common Language

The many African slaves that arrived on the shores of the Americas, and more specifically to what were the English (American) colonies, came with numerous languages. Although the West African Coast is recognized as the center of activity for the slave trade, slaves came from all across Africa, thanks in part to the cooperation and activities of different African tribes working with the hated slave traders. Therefore, many African languages and customs landed in the colonies. They were not segregated and grouped by language or culture, but were all thrown together into the melting pot of bondage.

There was no common language, but African slaves shared a familiar problem: bondage. African slaves were faced with a real dilemma. Survival was their most immediate problem and in order to do that, they had to develop ways and methods of communicating. To further complicate the matter, the slaves had to learn the language of their masters. Slaves were not allowed to be educated, so the task of learning the language (English) was made more difficult. At the same time, the inability to preserve the many languages and dialects of their varied tribal ancestry in some common lasting form, such as written records, doomed the many African cultures to disappear over time. The fact that there were so many different African cultures involved made it likely that only remnants of each would survive the transformation that was taking place. So, almost from the beginning, slavery was transforming Africans into a different culture-into a people fashioned from many different African languages and cultures. They were thrown together in a perpetual system of pain and servitude, a system which defined their lives not as people, but in terms of the property or possessions they had become.

The American slave came from many African ethnic groups. This happened on the plantations of America. Slavery was obviously very confusing to the Africans, who had previously been free in their homelands. These slaves were forced by their condition to develop a motivation to become a single people. Imagine what is happening here. They were forced to become a single people when in fact they were different people from the beginning. They were from different tribes and did not like each other. What a confusing way to begin to become a single people. This process was made more confusing by not sharing a common language.

By contrast, the Jewish slaves of ancient Egypt were from the outset a single people. They shared a common language and culture. They could also work from a more united effort in the cause of their freedom and welfare. Even though the Jews were in bondage, they were allowed to live as a people with their cultures intact and pass them on with complete records. The African slaves, in contrast, did not have a common culture or language from which to begin. His bondage was, therefore, much more taxing as he could only relate to his fellow slaves through his suffering. The African slaves were remnants of many different tribes who were forced by the lack of a common language to try to become a single people. Slavery was fashioning Africans from many different tribes, torn from their homelands, into a group, but not necessarily a homogeneous group. This was very different from the intensely tribal world of the African. The language that bonded these newly emerging but disenfranchised Americans on plantations across America was English. The English was crudely learned and vastly different from the native tongues it replaced.

Over time, the African got stronger with English. But what actually developed was a kind of English that was different from even the typical Northern and Southern English dialects spoken by Americans at the time. This "pigeon English" showed up later in Negro Spirituals and writings as uniquely Black and uniquely Black American. Many Black writings and especially Negro Spirituals are full of them. For example, the familiar song "Cum Bah Ya" is nothing more than a shortened old Negro version of the phrase "come by here."

The Negro version of English developed as it did because of the inability to educate slaves legally. The Africans or Negroes that were freed or escaped and lived in the non-slave North had a chance to learn the more correct version of English although not all were able to attend schools. Regardless of where or how the language was spoken, the new common language of the emerging Black Americans was now English.

Let us not forget to contrast this change and effect on the African slave in America to the mostly tribal existence of the native African who continued to exist virtually unchanged in his native homelands. The Blacks in America were being forced by their situation to abandon tribal rivalries in order to survive. The acceptance of a single common language was a great advantage in assisting this new forced cooperation between Blacks, slave and free. Also, in the native Africa, it was common to regard members of rival tribes as prey. The Blacks in America were being pulled into a cooperation that banded and bonded them into a recognized brotherhood, while the different dialects and languages continued unchanged in native Africa.

CHAPTER 3

Genetic Similarity

The Africans that landed in America, as numerous and tribally dispersed as they were, were similar in one obvious way. They all had common racial or genetic characteristics. What we need to understand here is that the societal forces that would act on the African in his new environment were destined to alter the genetic characteristics of the African slave. These factors include: intermarriage; escapes to freedom, which precipitated genetic intermingling with non-slave groups; and slaves being treated as property which often amounted to sexual predation and legalized rape. Over a period of time, the Africans in America would be very unlike their counterparts on the African continent.

The desire for freedom was an important driving force and one that did not come without some danger. Bondage was spiritually and physically depressing to the African slave and to the free Black. If they could be free, they could pursue a life of their own that included the ability to wed and have a family. This freedom was not just the goal of the male but also of the female. The slave culture existed alongside a free Black culture in the South as well as in the North. The desire for freedom inspired more than just a few slaves to attempt to escape and enjoy that cherished freedom. In so doing, many of the escaping slaves ended up settling with those who welcomed them as escapees. Oftentimes, these were Native American Indians or Europeans such as the French settlers who were not inclined to have slaves.

Intermarriage was frowned upon by basic White society everywhere. However, it did happen, and even if intermarriage did not occur, there began to arise a uniquely different group of Blacks who were neither true African nor White American. The fact that Blacks in most cases did not have rights meant that Whites, especially those who owned slaves, could take whatever liberties they wanted, which included sexual alliances, with their Black property. This engendered a system of legalized rape and sexual predation that created a Black middle race called mulattos that were neither White nor Black. The racial characteristics of these mulattos made them very recognizable from their typical African brothers. Those who were able to live free were left to themselves and often ostracized as unwanted bastards. Those sired by the White masters became house slaves or, conversely, often enjoyed privileged treatment. The products of White female indiscretions were often quickly hidden, done away with or sold off to new slave masters. Regardless of the circumstances of birth, the racial characteristics of the African in America began to change due to proximity and mixing with other races. In time these new people, more Black than White, would become recognizable not just by their appearance, but by their numbers.

In the free North, Blacks could actually live and build lives. Many Blacks thrived. There was a perceived preference for the more lightly complexioned Blacks. This actually created a jealously and dislike among the more traditionally darker-complexioned Blacks and their fairer-complexioned counterparts that still exists today in Black American society.

The lure of freedom also helped to change the unique racial characteristics of Blacks in America in another landmark manner. Many of the escaping and even free Africans went to live among and marry Native American Indians such as the Cherokee, Seminoles and other tribes that were slowly being engulfed or pushed off their traditional homelands. The Native American Indians often felt a kinship to the slaves as they, too, were being mistreated and minimally regarded by the growing White supremacy. There were similar unions being forged with the French of the

Louisiana Territory and to the far north in Canada. As westward expansion continued, the union of Blacks, Native Americans and Whites spread westward. Therefore, gradually, you see the racial characteristics typical to the African undergoing a change to reflect the unique racial character of a growing American melting pot.

Meanwhile, if we look back to the African Continent, even though the continent itself is being increasingly impacted by the presence of Europeans, the basic genetic characteristics of the native African remain generally unaffected, unlike the American Black culture. Economically deprived and victimized, the native African was basically excluded in his own country, but remained virtually genetically unchanged. This was not true in America. Both free Black and slave cultures began to undergo genetic changes that, over time, rendered the American Black very different in appearance, character and genetics from his counterpart on the African continent.

CHAPTER 4

Social Order & Traditions
Define a Culture

The experience of slavery in America actually was responsible for creating two Black cultures, one slave and one free. Though these two cultures were in many ways at odds with each other, they had one thing in common: they were isolated and cut off from mainstream American society. With necessity being the mother of invention, for survival's sake, the Negroes had to fashion a culture made up of ethnic fusion. Compounding the problem of creating a culture and passing it on were the increased numbers of slaves pouring into the southern United States from the slavery pipeline. These new arrivals continued to originate from many different tribes and to bring just as many different traditions and customs. In the vast African homeland, the different tribes were at least free to pass along their customs, practices and traditions. That was not true for the enslaved Africans in America.

Even free Blacks were not spared from this difficulty of growing and passing along a matured culture. They did not have access to mechanisms such as public records nor the status of importance to command such an expectation.

Once they arrived in America, the African lost his African name, which right away deprived him of much of his heritage. Losing his name deprived the African of an essential part of his culture, his past, and past generations. The name also spoke to the character of an individual. Without his name and without his freedom, the African was immediately handicapped. Even those slaves who were fortunate enough to experience freedom were not spared this condition. They were cut off, separated and had to fashion a new life and new ways within this new land. They were broken remnants who lived lives that existed as such.

Other factors also made it difficult for the Africans to sustain their African culture and to assist in developing a new and indigenous Black culture in America. One such factor was illiteracy. African slaves were denied the ability to read and write. That denial was one of the horrible debilitating laws of slavery. This virtually doomed the many African cultures that were thrown together because they could not pass on their traditions or their culture. Indeed, much of their culture was already lost because of the way they were thrown into slavery with others of different origins. While there were segments or fragments of those African cultures preserved in some traditions and incorporated into the newly emerging Black culture based on English as the spoken language, the inability to write and keep records would ensure the eventual loss of even those. The endeavors needed to pass along a culture were replaced with the harsh reality of surviving the inhuman yoke of slavery. Much of the Africans' history just disappeared. Professor Sterling Stuckey has written prolifically on African slave culture and is a good source of reference. The loss of mobility coupled with the large scale inability to read and write dealt a heavy blow to sustaining a culture. Restricted mobility meant that Black culture in America was limited in its ability to replicate itself.

But one factor did emerge as a unifying force: Christianity. Christianity became a unifying factor that strongly influenced the learning/acceptance of English as a common language. The growth of Christianity and learning English helped to bring about the disappearance of tribal influences. We began to see the emergence of a uniquely American Black culture. Even so, this culture was hampered by the inability to read and write and keep records. Slavery, in all its cruelty, was beginning to transform African slaves into a single people, the American Black. This was born out of the slaves' predicament and a need to cooperate. This was very different from the intensely tribal existence of the continental African in his native environment.

It was not that the Africans did not have their own forms of religion; certainly they did. It was a definite contrast to the Christianity being learned by the thousands of Blacks in America. The acceptance of Christianity by the thousands of Africans over generations helped to create a kind of *indigenous* Black race of Americans. Their Christianity was unifying in that it was born out of suffering and championed the coming of a better day and time for slaves and Black Americans.

Learning a single language over decades also created a cultural togetherness for the emerging Black Americans. As this occurred over several generations of Africans, this cultural togetherness was a feat that was not duplicated in the Africans' native homeland on the African continent. As noted earlier, the existence there was still tribal and separate. This cultural melding of many ethnic groups into one English-speaking cultural group who practiced the beliefs of Christianity was a tremendous feat for the emerging Black Americans. Their suffering was great, but their ability to survive was greater. That ability to adapt and survive began a metamorphosis that would eventually culminate in a vastly different African, generations later, from he who had landed on the shores of the southern

United States: an African that was less African and more Black American because of the impact of the changes brought on by the experience of slavery. The African was transformed and what emerged was an indigenous Black race born under the weight of slavery. This indigenous Black became known as the American Negro, who was part slave, part African, part American Indian, part Caucasian, part free and completely forged on American soil. These Black Americans reflect and resemble their varied ancestry.

To reiterate, a highly mixed African culture landed on the shores of America. It consisted of what the African slaves could salvage of their own different cultures and the culture forged by the bonds of slavery. The Africans went from many languages to a single language. They became converts to Christianity. The impact of intermarriage with other ethnic groups brought changes. The inability to read and write and the lack of freedom to pass along an African culture over time yielded a Black indigenous culture that was different from the highly mixed African culture that had landed in America—and understandably so.

CHAPTER 5

The Family Unit as a Stabilizing Factor

In every culture, the family unit has always been a key factor to the survival of that culture or racial group. It began very differently for the Africans that arrived in America as slaves. There was no family unit. Right away, this demonstrates a very big difference between the African slave and the typical immigrant who brought his family with him or, very soon afterwards, the family was able to follow. The African slave had no such opportunity. So we can see that even the African family unit, that most essential foundation for sustaining a culture, began in disarray and disunity and had to be built from often competing or combative cultures. The African slaves did not have the benefit of whole families or the promise or hope of uniting a family later.

In assessing the Black family unit under slavery, it is important to recognize that even though a family unit eventually did emerge, it was born of confusion, and even though there was genetic similarity, cultural and tribal differences abounded. The African slave family unit was born in instability. Because of the limiting boundaries of slavery, a stable family unit was not possible. The issue is whether the Black family unit that emerged under slavery was effectively capable of sustaining the African culture that was transplanted in America. Because of the limitations they faced, the Black family units that emerged were not very effective in stabilizing or passing on a unified culture.

We must first recognize that there were two emerging Black cultures within the shores of the United States. One was free, and the other was slave. Even though one existed free and the other in bondage, they still suffered from similar problems. They were both generally cut off from mainstream American society, existing in separate communities. The impacts on the Black family unit were felt by both Black segments in America. Some of the results of these impacts on Black America can be seen even today. The lack of a clear identity as a people is a problem. Often, there is an absence of strong unifying traditions that tie families and their histories together as in other races.

While it is true that the Black family unit did exist, again the question is how stable was it and how effective was it in preserving and establishing a unified and identifiable Black culture, slave or free. The Black family unit in America during and after slavery was basically unstable for decades. The instability was not inherent in Black families but due to the nature of the institution of slavery. The Black family unit in America during slavery was not set up to sustain a culture, but to accommodate slavery and provide labor. The slaves were encouraged to have large families in order to sustain a free labor source. Not only were they encouraged to have large families, they were even bred for labor and sold according to the needs or whims of the slave masters. This meant that families could be broken up and children and parents separated, often at will. This meant that children were often not aware of parentage. Males were firmly dominated and carefully held in check as a means of controlling and dominating the race. Infidelity was expected and even encouraged within the system of fragmented family structures that developed under the influence of slavery.

Into this cauldron, you have thousands of Africans pouring into America from differing tribes and cultures and all bringing bits and pieces of their lost lives with them. They were faced with the prospect of beginning again to build a life not as a family member, but as a newly acquired slave and as property. What developed from this forced system of labor, isolation, illiteracy and broken lives certainly cannot be called stable family life. Nor did it grow and sustain a culture with a clear identity and direction. As a matter of fact, it was just the opposite. The culture that developed was very much lacking an identity and was generated out of a basic survival need. Add to this mosaic the practice of breeding slaves for labor, the complete deprivation of bondage, and the slave's intense desire to be free, and it is clear that Blacks in America had a much more pressing issue, and that was survival.

Now it can be argued, and with some justification, that there was in America a free Black culture of families and learned scholars that existed along with Caucasian America. These Black families and scholars were productive, literate and contributed to the societies in which they lived. Some were well-known and fought for freedom and the assimilation of Blacks into the fabric of the United States. But we must remember that these families and free Blacks were themselves tied to slavery, split families and partial or lost family histories. In addition, they were suffering from the same malady that affected Black slaves, which was isolation from the mainstream of American society. They were unable to mount a large following of their own kind in order to affect a meaningful ethnic movement to unite and change the fortunes of Blacks in America. Indeed, they were often divided among themselves, as history shows, as to what path or action to take. For example, some espoused the idea of returning to Africa, while others wanted to be separate and equal. Others desired assimilation into American society.

A Black family unit did develop in both free and slave Black America, but that family unit was unable to produce a unified Black culture with a clear and strong identity. What existed were basically separate remnants that were split and far from being unified in purpose. Contributing to this reality were the factors of isolation, illiteracy, instability, selling slaves, separating families, and the intense yearning for freedom by Blacks. But to be sure, a Black ethnic group did emerge, but it was a race of people without a clear history or identity, lacking togetherness. Racial and cultural pride had been lost under the stigma of slavery.

CHAPTER 6

The Ability to Pass on
Heritage & Culture

One of the real misconceptions here is that America enslaved a single nation of Black people. That is far from the truth. Yes, the slaves were all black and from the African continent. Beyond that, they were from different tribes and different countries and spoke many dialects. Since they carried only bits and pieces of their native cultures, it was difficult to pass anything along. Of course, I understand that there were many slaves from the same country who spoke the same language, but, remember, this was slavery. What were the chances they would end up in the same place, and even if they did, they were dumped into an environment with hundreds of other slaves with the same problem—survival. They found themselves in a system of servitude and hard labor and not in a situation that was conducive to replicating a culture. The inability to communicate was a tremendous barrier. Learning a common language took time and not being allowed to read and write made it even more difficult.

There were remnants of many African cultures. Since slaves were not taught to read and write there were not many ways that these remnants could be preserved. Some were written in native tongues, carvings or whatever mediums that could serve as an effective manner to pass along anything of large-scale significance.

It can be argued that the free Blacks, many of whom could read and write, had the ability to preserve and pass along their culture and heritage. It must be remembered that many of those free Blacks were at one time themselves slaves and what they had to pass along was buried largely in the remnants of their experience in slavery. In the cases where there were records, they were incomplete and largely kept in family Bibles, poorly written, and in the heads of the people. Blacks, both free and slave, were not very highly regarded as people, and there was no real focused effort by society at large to have effective mechanisms to record and pass along the heritage of Black people. The African culture in America was doomed from the outset because of the inability of the African to transplant his culture in this country.

CHAPTER 7

Perspective

This is a good place to try to put all that I have said up to this point in perspective. I started out by rejecting the accepted contention that we are African Americans. By definition, an African American is someone who, by his own volition, comes to this country and goes through the process of becoming an American citizen. It is a voluntary process, and it takes approximately seven years to complete. The Africans who do this are born in Africa, emigrate willingly and change citizenship in the same vein. They do not identify themselves with Black Americans and their history of slavery. They are different by birth, character and orientation. The Black Americans' experience is totally different. Choice was not one of their options. They have been here and a part of this country for centuries and have known no other homeland. The Emancipation Proclamation freed us of enforced bondage and made us Americans officially. Even though the Emancipation Proclamation did not go far enough in protecting our freedom and citizenship, our history is part of the fabric of this country. We went into slavery as African slaves or "Black Ivory," as we were called by slave traders. We emerged centuries and changes later as Black Americans. The African was transformed, and what emerged was the American Negro, an indigenous Black race. The American Negro was part slave, part free, part African, part Caucasian, part American Indian, part French, English, Spanish and completely forged in slavery and on the American continent. We have more than earned the right to be called Black Americans.

This evolution took place here in America. The change did not take place overnight. It took centuries and a lot of events to make it happen. It did not occur in a vacuum, separated from the history of other Americans or even America itself. Some of the same factors that helped to shape this country also played a part in the development and evolution of Black Americans. For instance, the opposition to slavery pitted this country, North and South, in a bitter and devastating Civil War. The effect on the country and Americans, White and Black, is undeniable even though much of the history and its effect on Black Americans have been selectively excluded in the history of the United States.

The economic growth of America before and after the Civil War is chronicled in the history of these

United States and much of it is grounded and founded on the labor provided by Black Americans. This selective exclusion is part of the burden Blacks face in coming to grips with our place in American society. As is the case with most Americans, Black Americans came from somewhere else to become what we are.

Slavery is one of the greatest shames of America. In the preceding pages, I have attempted to show how it affected both slave and free Black Americans in the time leading up to the twentieth century. The African went into slavery, and what evolved from the experience was not an African, but a Black American, forged in bondage and shaped by all the different forces acting on him to produce what is a reflection of and a product of America's past, the Black American. The African was doomed from the outset and not able to transplant his culture in the land he was brought to serve. What did evolve, however, was the Black American. He was sturdy, resilient and as uniquely American as his spirituals or his jazz, and as we shall speak about later, contributed to all phases of making this country great.

We are Black Americans and not African Americans. The term African American not only does not fit us, it is by definition an incorrect presentation of who we are as a people. It not only clouds the issue of who we are, but masks a shame (slavery) that we as a people have not been able to cast off and has prevented us from standing up and taking our rightful place in America.

CHAPTER 8

The Problem

The question arises, if we are Black Americans and not African Americans as I contend, then why have we not risen up and asserted that belief and ended this cycle of confusion? I believe there are a great many Black people who believe, as I do, that we are Americans who just happen to be Black and live as such and have for a long time. The reality is that they, like me, long ago tired of the pendulum swing of confusion and while not being really apathetic, knew of no real way to say what we felt and have, like the silent majority, just been inclined to live our lives as we believed. I have shouted loudly within myself as I have watched us go from Negroes to Afro Americans, to Blacks (which we thought made a lot of sense) to the African American tag. When will this nonsense cease? Can none of us realize who and what we are and stay with it? The reality is we (Black people in America) have always had an identity problem. It is inherent in the way we came into being. Yet I believe that if you asked most Black Americans if they think we have an identity problem, they will say no. As you can see, I disagree.

The end of the Civil War and the Emancipation Proclamation made us free Americans but that was really about all. There was little serious effort to bring us into the fabric of America even though there were credible efforts in some areas of the country. Some Blacks became officials and part of the government though they were doomed to failure as the country was more about healing the wounds of five years of Civil War than dealing with a large group of freedmen who knew little about being part of a democracy, let alone faring well in it.

The period of reconstruction was about bringing the South back into the federal union. It was not about Blacks, and their issues as Blacks would be sold out at every juncture to placate or reclaim the South. Political actions reflecting the attitude of the "Three Fifths Compromise" of 1887 were still around to insure the interests of Blacks would be sold out during the period of reconstruction. That same mentality carried over into the early twentieth century. The D. W. Griffith portrayal of Blacks as an evil menace to White America that needed to be stamped out in his movie *The Birth of A Nation* represented the attitude of the nation regarding Blacks. Not only did it portray Black people as evil, but it glorified the Ku Klux Klan as the saviors of the nation and Caucasian Americans. In this climate, the power structure did not exist for the interests of Black people to gain ascendancy.

The end of the Civil War set Black Americans adrift and divided amid a sea of confusion and corruption. We were divided and without any real identity as a people, except being Negro and free. There was no leadership to bring the fragments together in unity or to deal with the problems of a newly freed people. We were not prepared to become productive citizens. We were divided among ourselves, the free Blacks and the newly freed Blacks. As a people, we were doomed to failure just as much as the slaves before us had been doomed in their efforts to be free and to transplant their culture. We were doomed because we had no central underlying unity nor the political structure and power base to be successful.

From where was our identity to stem? Was it to come from the free Blacks who were a growing number before emancipation who longed for freedom and assimilation into mainstream American society? Was it to come from the large number of field hands or laborers across the South who were largely illiterate and denied access to American society? Was it to come from the mulatto or Blacks of mixed parentage who were outcasts from their White relatives and shunned by many

Blacks? Was it to come from the runaway who had escaped and found freedom and a new life as an American Indian, French or whatever he had settled into?

Over the years that followed, there were many competing philosophies that flourished in one way or the other with differing degrees of strength. There was the Back to Africa movement that took shape under Marcus Garvey. There was the separate, though not exactly equal, posture of Booker T. Washington and his followers. Both of these efforts conflicted with the desire to be equal and assimilated into the American mainstream, which was the goal of many free Blacks that populated the free northern states prior to and after the Civil War. The great masses of freed Blacks in the southern states were more preoccupied with surviving under Jim Crow laws and avoiding lynching, constant reminders of their precarious condition.

Without strong, central, unified leadership to pull the divided factions of young Black America together amid the corruption and confusion that existed in a country that did nothing to protect and ensure the welfare of its new Americans, we (Black Americans) drifted without identity and mostly without direction. It would take the Civil Rights movement of the mid-twentieth century and the emergence of a strong, unifying leader in the person of Dr. Martin Luther King, Jr. to pull Black leaders together as a unifying force and give structure, direction and a voice to Black Americans. Up to that time, there were many manifestations of Blacks trying to assert themselves and gain our rightful place. The conditions were not right for those efforts to succeed. We did not have the access to the methods nor the political or social clout for those efforts to be successful. Whether it was wearing an afro hair style or a dashiki, following the likes of W. E. B. DuBois or Jessie Jackson, we were seeking to establish an identity and a sense of unity and belonging.

The years following the Civil War and freedom were necessary formative years, many of them spent drifting aimlessly, searching for acceptance, fighting for survival and equality as we sifted through the baggage of our existence trying desperately to establish and understand who we were.

The well-known author, Alex Haley, who wrote the book *Roots* was driven by his desire to understand who he was. That book and TV mini-series spawned a whole new movement by Americans, and not just Black Americans, searching for their identity. When you consider how Black Americans came into being and that many of us face the reality of broken racial and family history, it should be understandable why we have sought to understand our roots. We need that closure in order to go forward as proud people.

Family reunions, which have seen a rebirth and

growth among Black Americans, can be seen as another manifestation of Blacks' search for who we are. Today, many of the family reunions in Black America have been seen to reach out and include the Caucasian side of their lineage. This shows how difficult it is to separate Black and White history in this country, especially in what is known as the South. Our history is racially interwoven.

Having an identity crisis did not mean there were no successful Black individuals or Black endeavors. Between the Emancipation Proclamation and the Civil Rights Movement, there were many Blacks who distinguished themselves, especially during Reconstruction, when we had prominent blacks in governmental roles. But that soon gave way to the widespread corruption and Jim Crow politics of the time. Because Blacks were denied access to the same rights and privileges enjoyed by their White counterparts many of the successful Black figures, like W. E. B. Dubois spent much of their lives abroad where they enjoyed more notoriety and acceptance.

There were even successful Black settlements that flourished, but died untimely and cruel deaths because Black success was not looked upon with acceptance by White America. Such settlements as Rosewood in northeast Florida and Black Wall Street of Tulsa, Oklahoma were destroyed by angry White mobs.

These atrocities stand as a testament to the shame of America's own holocaust and failure of this country's effort to protect the rights of all Americans. American history between the Civil War and the birth of the Civil Rights movement of the mid-fifties, which was to change America, is ripe with great endeavors and distinguished Black effort, which I will speak about in summation later.

CHAPTER 9

Baggage

Slavery carries a shame that Black Americans in general have not been able to erase. Many will, in fact, have difficulty accepting my contention that slavery is the birth mother of the Black American. But how can it be explained otherwise? Today, we call ourselves African Americans, but the real truth is that there is a big difference between the Africans that are today pouring into this country and seek to become U.S. citizens and ourselves as Black Americans. I have invested a lot of pages to show logically and rationally that we are not African Americans. To call ourselves African Americans is, in fact, a contradiction for all native-born Black Americans.

As a collegian at Northwestern University, I had the opportunity to attend school with a number of African students. In my association with them, even though we were cordial and friendly, they each made it very clear that they were African or Nigerian or French or a native of their country of origin. They were quick to point out that they were different from the Black Americans or the American Negro, as they called us then. They were always quick to point out that they had never been slaves as we had been. They regarded the slavery as a stigma attached to the Black American and made it very clear that it was a difference they regarded as negative. My experience with our African classmates left a lasting impression upon me and made it clear that I could not put native Africans and Black Americans in the same pot. We are different and come from different places and experiences. While we can relate to each other and live in the same place, it is quite clear that we are of different worlds and the events that shaped us will not allow us to stand side by side as the same people. That does not mean that we hate or dislike each other; it just means we are different. It stands to reason that for me to claim to be something I am not is a conflict with who I am, and if who I am carries a stigma that even the people I claim to be like do not accept, then the conflict is obviously with me.

The burden of slavery is not the only baggage incurred by Black Americans as we have traveled the road into the twenty-first century. Attached to the stigma of slavery were other fallacies that we have had to contend with as Black people that have exacerbated our burden. Blacks were often said to be ignorant, lazy and irresponsible, incapable, and had low family or moral values. Obviously, it was necessary to do this to paint the picture that was needed to show that Blacks were not deserving of standing equal to Whites. Let us look briefly as to what purpose this served.

"Ignorant"

Remember that slaves were a warrior people even though they were taken from many different tribes and countries. That meant that unless they were kept under a very suppressive and brutal system and denied the ability to learn and grow as normal people, they would rise up and revolt. Therefore, it was necessary to keep them suppressed and illiterate. Yet there were scores of slaves who learned to read and write even though they could not use it openly. As for the Blacks who were literate, including those in freedom, they had little or no power to change very much. Even after the Emancipation Proclamation, the fact is that America was not prepared to deal with new Americans, their numbers, their diverse makeup and the large amount of illiteracy. Therefore, it was easy to do nothing and allow the existing stereotype to continue as fact even though there were living examples all around that attested to the ability of Blacks to learn and prosper.

"Lazy and Irresponsible"

How else would you characterize slaves? You certainly would not refer to them as industrious, capable and filled with tons of initiative and leadership capability. Yet these lazy and irresponsible people were central to building a very large part of a growing country: the backbone of labor. Some even found time to distinguish themselves though they received little note. Black Americans have a rich history. As we dig through the real facts of American history, we can find initiative and achievement even before the exploits of Crispus Attucks, who enjoys widespread fame as one of the first to die in the cause of American independence.

"Incapable"

This characteristic is also part of the necessity to suppress and humiliate a warrior race. It was necessary to put forth theories that supported Blacks as an inferior race, incapable of standing as equals to their White brethren. To do otherwise would be to accept equality of Blacks and Whites, and that would not support slavery. Blacks were a problem that America was not ready to, or even prepared to, deal with. Therefore, any theory that provided a basis to support doing nothing was another justification for doing nothing about the condition of Negroes in America. The bottom line was that Emancipation did not free Blacks. It only removed the tag of illegal bondage. The years between the Emancipation Proclamation and the passage of the Civil Rights Act of 1964 was a period of gross irresponsibility for America in honoring the foundations of the Constitution as far as Blacks were concerned. These years were full of open bigotry, hatred, and jealousy. Many manifestations of the industriousness of Blacks as capable people were generally ignored, regarded as out of the ordinary (flukes) or destroyed through violence and lynching as was done in the cases of Tulsa's Black Wall Street in Oklahoma or Florida's Rosewood. To view Blacks as capable people was socially, politically, and economically unacceptable. Efforts by Blacks to "stand as equals" were quickly put down as insurrections.

"No Family Values"

I have already discussed how important family was to the survival of Blacks in slavery. Black families were not easily preserved or protected in pre- and post-Civil War America. It is interesting to note that in order to support slavery and keep free labor to build a major part of this country, Blacks were urged to be prolific and have large families even though these families were often split apart or sold off. Blacks were even bred like animals to produce a stream of strong labor for the fields and plantations of the South. Of this I can attest, as in my family history passed along to us, my own great, great grandfather was used as a stud and taken from plantation to plantation to breed with Black women. This was acceptable as long as it was being done to support the institution of slavery. As a people, however, imagine what it must have been like to live with your family being split up, or to try and have a family in a system that openly encouraged and condoned promiscuity and infidelity. Slavery was not about supporting or building family values—it was about labor.

When slavery was abolished and White America was faced with accepting former slaves as equals, suddenly this behavior that had been forced on a helpless people was now used against them as being a negative part of their character.

Obviously, these characterizations were self-serving to those who had an interest in maintaining the status quo and continuing to deny Black people their Constitutional rights. At the same time, it was detrimental to a young and emerging ethnic group who had been born in confusion and suffered from the stigma of slavery that even native Africans found objectionable. This complexity deepened the identity crisis that plagued Black people of African descent. For such a young ethnic group, largely illiterate and without much accumulated wealth or a political base, being denied access at all turns, it is understandable why we would come into the twentieth century with a lot of baggage. It is also understandable why we would have an identity crisis. Paul Robeson was known to say, "You cannot assume a nationality as you would a suit of clothes." He meant that it is important and proper to know what it means to be of that nationality. Depicting ourselves as African Americans is in conflict with that very concept.

CHAPTER 10

The Name Things

One of the popular thoughts and positions among some Black Americans, especially those who have set themselves apart from the mainstream of Black America, is that the names we have are slave names. Names such as Campbell, Johnson, Warren, Alexander and many others identify us as slaves' descendents. Groups of people such as the well-known Black Muslims have chosen to give up their given names and selected Muslim names. These names, they feel, give them an identity with which they are more comfortable.

From my perspective, I fail to understand how this is anything more than another form of escapism and search for an identity that links to something other than slavery. Does it provide a salve that erases the slavery stigma? Does it eliminate the reality that they are inescapably a part of their slave ancestors? Does it offer an identity that separates them from the resistance within their own relatives and family? More importantly, does it solve the very real problem of who we are as Black

Americans? No! It does not. It is simply another manifestation of how important it is for us to once and for all establish our own real identity. It is like the dashiki, the Afro hair style, or the Afro American designation that preceded the African American designation. These movements continue to reflect the nature of our origin. Our origin began in confusion, separation, fragmentation and devoid of much real racial and cultural oneness except for the need to survive.

We have already dealt with how the African slave lost his name. Slavery came with a new language and new names (such as Campbell, Johnson and Alexander), that were identifiable by the slave owners they were attached to. This was very important, for as property, they could not be identified by their given names. Their new language was English, and over the years and centuries that followed, these new Black Americans had to not only rebuild lives from scratch with fragments like themselves, but they had to build the character and identity of their borrowed names. These new Americans, over the years and centuries to come, gave character to those borrowed names. Our names, like our heritage, are a testament to our durability. They should be a source of pride for, like so much of what we as Black Americans share, we earned them.

CHAPTER 11

The Solution

I have stated my case, and it is very gratifying to have done so. I have also tried to remain true to my intent to be rational, logical and thoughtful. I believe there are many out there who share my belief. We know who we are and have come to grips with our past. We have moved on. We are proud of who we are and what we have accomplished. Over the years, we have endured all these identity swings quietly. These are the people about whom I write. We are finally drawing a definitive line in the sand. This is where we get off. We choose to stand correctly as the people we are: Black Americans.

The desire to be free and equal inspired many noteworthy efforts through out the eighteenth, nineteenth and twentieth centuries by Americans of color and others hoping to free Blacks in America beyond the shackles of slavery and Emancipation. Efforts were aimed at helping Black Americans find their rightful place in American society. They all had degrees of success, but failed to unite Black Americans, primarily because we were not ready. As an ethnic group, we were still a young people and needed to grow into what we were to become. A key part of that growth was literacy. Another was to develop and gain a political base of power such as was provided by the Civil Rights Amendment and the Voting Rights Act. Without these important foundations and a commitment from our government to enforce them, we had no foundational power to achieve much. It is said that nothing happens before its time. The coming of the mid-Fifties and the Civil Rights movement was the culmination of a lot of growth.

In making my points, I have focused heavily on the evils of slavery. I do not know if I am ready to say there is anything good about it, but there were some positives that have served Black people well. First, there was the bonding together of a people who, while not yet united as a people or in their efforts, did share a common goal. That common goal was the desire for freedom. It was a driving force for free Blacks and those sentenced to live as slaves. The free Blacks longed to be a part of America, and slaves longed to be free. Both were seeking freedom from their own form of enslavement. That drive to be free and whole would help fashion a people.

Christianity was a healing and comforting factor that provided hope and optimism to Blacks, who would ultimately be freed from their bondage. It would also lay the foundation for patience and endurance that would eventually play a part in the most significant occurrence in two centuries for Black people, the Civil Rights movement. It took Martin Luther King, Jr. himself a Christian minister, to awaken the conscience of America to finally apportion Constitutional rights and freedom to Black people in America. This was a non-violent movement supported by Christian principles.

Contrary to popular stereotypes, Black people did have a deep sense of family and good moral values. They fought great odds to build families and hold them together. They endured hardships, separations and blatant laxity from a government sworn to uphold and preserve the rights of its people. But then Blacks were not generally regarded as people. They were a problem left to America by the Emancipation Proclamation at the end of the Civil War.

Let us not forget that even though they were contained and generally denied access, there was a large free Black population above the Mason-Dixon Line. Against great odds, these free people of color did make significant progress in building families even though some were themselves escaped slaves who left family back in slavery.

Finally, slavery left an enduring resilience to bend but not break while surviving this country's inhumanity to man until the gestation period of the deliverance of Blacks in America was at hand. These hard earned but positive imprints of slavery served Black people well in their journey and fight for equality.

In spite of the fact that we are a young ethnic group, I find a lot to be proud of as I survey the history of Black people in America. Our history is ripe with struggle, yes; disunity, yes; and I have tried valiantly to provide a picture of why that disunity has been present. If you are inclined to be ashamed of who you are, then no amount of writing and facts will change that. However, for me pride began early in life as my parents instilled in me, that being Black was not a disgrace, but something to be proud of. The history books have been selective in what is accorded to Blacks, but as I have peeled back the covers of American history, I have found that it is rich with Black achievement. These achievements serve as a source of pride for me in a people who started from slavery, demonstrating that even in bondage we could stand with pride.

Let us start with the fact that there is no denying that Black labor helped to build this country. Cotton may have been king in Dixie but the labor was obviously Black. Ironically, the first recorded casualty of the American Revolution, known as the Boston Massacre, was a Black man. He was Crispus Attucks. We have all read about Sojourner Truth, who risked her life to free Black slaves. We also know about Booker

T. Washington and George Washington Carver were a few who made the history books in America. What has inspired me is the amount of information that is not in the history books about the accomplishments of Black people. This information supports the fact that Blacks have been prominent in all phases of American history and life. The evidence is there for those who want to know.

We have read how Caucasians fought and died in sacrifice to preserve our nation. Black Americans also fought in every major war throughout the history of the United States. One hundred eighty-six thousand Black soldiers fought in the Civil War. Thirty-eight thousand died. Some of us have seen the movie *Glory* about the 54th Massachusetts, an all-Black regiment that distinguished itself during the Civil War. The contributions of the "Buffalo Soldiers" of the all-Black 9th and 10th cavalries are now slowly coming to light and the part that they played in the settling of the West and particularly the southwestern United States. The Native Americans had great respect for the fighting spirit of these "Buffalo Soldiers" as they named them. These same soldiers were key players in the Indian wars of the western United States and even came to the rescue of General George Armstrong Custer who campaigned against granting voting rights to these Americans and refused to command them as soldiers.

How could we not be proud of the contributions of the Tuskegee Airmen who patrolled the skies over Europe, and out-fought and out-flew the best that Hitler had to offer? The Red Ball Express, many of them Black, supplied the American Army with precious supplies in the face of enemy opposition. The 24th Infantry, the most decorated unit of the Korean War, was one of the "Buffalo Soldier" infantry units established prior to President Truman's order to integrate the Armed Forces. Inspection of the more than fifty thousand names on the Vietnam Memorial Wall in Washington D.C. will find that Black Americans more than carried their fair load.

I find pride in the knowledge now available to me that has let me know that as Americans moved West, often as many as two of every five cowboys were Black. Some, like Bill Pickett and Ben Hodges, even found time to become well known. Ben Hodges, a Black gambler, was as well known in Dodge City as Wyatt Earp. One of the more famous cattle drive trails was named for a Black man, the Goodnight Loving Trail. Mary Fields, better known as "Stagecoach Mary," hauled freight and delivered mail and was as seasoned a frontiersman as Black Pony Express rider William Robinson.

There have been women in our history like famed aviatrix and the first licensed Black pilot, Bessie Coleman. Educators like Mary McLeod Bet.hune have graced our history and enriched our efforts, as did Althea Gibson, tennis champion. The first Black Congresswoman, Shirley Chisholm, served with distinction and was a revered politician.

Dr. Daniel Hale Williams was one of the first Americans to perform heart surgery and was a pioneer in the field of medicine. In the field of entertainment and the arts, we have been richly blessed with personalities like Paul Robeson, known internationally for his work. Bill Robinson, renowned dancer, and Lena Horne, vocalist and actress, paved the way for stars like Sidney Poitier and Harry Belafonte. As Black people, we have given the world art forms such as the Negro Spiritual, jazz music and what is known as the Blues.

In the area of human rights, the list of contributors is long and often sadly sacrificial as their efforts ended in their deaths at the hands of assassins whose sole purpose was to silence their voices and the impact they were having on organizing one of the largest minorities in the history of this country, Black people. People like Medgar Evers and Martin Luther King, Jr. Politically, people like Ralph Bunche and the already mentioned Congresswoman Shirley Chisholm, Coleman Young as first Black mayor of a major U.S. city showed that Blacks were capable statesmen. So did Andrew Young, the first Black Ambassador to the United Nations.

There are many others. The list of Black achievement would be exhaustive if I went back through history and listed them and their accomplishments, but for the sheer sake of impact and information I will just list some of them and their contributions to demonstrate my meaning. These are people who have had, and continue to have, an impact and an effect on our daily lives. Many of us are not even aware that these contributors are Black:

INVENTION	BLACK INVENTOR
The Refrigerator	John Standard
The Shoe Lasting Machine	John Matzelinger
The Fountain Pen & the Hand Stamp	W.B. Purvis
The Electric Lamp	Joseph Nichols and Lewis Lattimer
The Gas Mask and Traffic Light	Garrett Morgan
Railway Telegraphy	Grandville Woods
The Rotary Engine	Andrew Beard
Air Conditioning Unit	Frederick Jones
The Typewriter	Lee Burridge
The Elevator	Alexander Mils
The Automatic Gear Shift (cars)	Richard Spikes
The Electric Trolley	Elbert R. Robinson
The Street Sweeper	Charles Brooks
The Pencil Sharpener	John Love

The Postmarking Machine	William Barry
The Letter Drop	Phillip Downing
The Lawn Sprinkler	Joseph Smith
The Lawn Mower	John Burr
The Heating Furnace	Alice Parker
The Ironing Board	Sarah Boone
The Clothes Dryer	George T. Sammons

As I indicated, I could go on and on with evidence that is there for Black people today to pull up their history and learn about our accomplishments. They go far beyond the mayhem and bad images that are paraded before us each day by the news media and TV, images that perpetuate stereotypes and keep us just as the slaves we used to be, ignorant of our past and therefore unable to determine our future. If we succumb to those images and that rhetoric and not to the evidence before us today, as more of us continue to build lives for ourselves in mainstream America as full-fledged American, and not Africans who happen to be Americans, then we will not achieve our manifest destiny as Black Americans. Blacks are not all Democrats. We are increasingly Republican and Independents and even millionaires. What we have not achieved is the kind of unity and togetherness that will allow us to become the political power we could be if we were of an accord.

CHAPTER 12

Conclusion

When I started out, some time ago now, to vent my frustration at being referred to by a name that does not really fit me and that by definition is incorrect, African American, I was not sure where it would take me. I had an outline and a conviction and that outline has undergone many modifications, but the conviction has remained. I am not an African American. I am a Black American of African descent who, by progression, bears little resemblance, with the exception of skin color, to the African slaves that were my ancestors. Slavery was my birth mother(as a people), and over the years the Black American that emerged from slavery is vastly different from the African that went into slavery. As Black Americans, we do not know what it is to be an African, just as the African does not know what it means to be a Black American. We walked different paths to get to where we are. Yet the African can be proud of who he is, and we should be just as proud of who we are.

Yes, we were once slaves and make no mistake about it, the African, because of his tribal orientation, played a large part in supporting that slavery. As we progressed from slave to emancipation to freedmen and to American citizen, we have shed many shackles and still carry many burdens from that experience. But as I stated, we are a young ethnic group, and we are still growing into what we will become. As we bear those burdens today, we face many new ones as the world we live in becomes more multinational. What about the thousands of new Africans today who are pouring into this country? How do we characterize them? What are they to be called? Are they Black Americans? I do not think so. More importantly, what about those millions of us who have never seen Africa except through the world of knowledge, whose ancestors were Black, White, European, French, German, Jewish and Native American, who have been a part of this country for centuries? Is it correct to call ourselves African American? I have spent a considerable amount of time and effort saying, "I think it is not correct."

Ultimately, our pride comes from within us and our conviction also from within to be okay with who we are. I am okay with who I am, a proud Black American. I come from a rich and proud tradition of overcoming with achievement. I choose to focus on those things that are positive about who we are and from where we came. The foolishness has gone on long enough: we are here, and we ain't going anywhere. We have paid for our slice of this pie with our sweat, our blood, our sacrifice, and our achievements. We are currently in another metamorphosis. There is much more to come.

A Proud Black American
—wlc

CHAPTER 13

Retrospective

Now that I have taken the time to explore an issue that I believe to be totally relevant to the identity of Black Americans of African descent, I would like to complicate things even further. In the preceding pages I passionately and rationally debated the reasons that we (those of us who descended from African slaves and make up the majority of the Black population in the United States) should not be called African Americans. I believe those reasons to be sound and support them as I have argued.

Today, however, there are thousands of native Africans and native Caribbean Islanders that are pouring into the United States and call America home. They, too, are part of the large and varied group of people of color commonly referred to by the designation African Americans. Beyond that, Black Americans, Africans and Islanders have very little in common with each other. This creates an interesting parallel to the problem that the African slaves originally faced when brought to this country. What will it take to become a unifying force? Black people in America today are facing the same problem that began in slavery, only this time there is no bondage and the problem is on a much grander scale.

The African, the Islander and the Black American are culturally different and share dissimilar backgrounds and histories that make it very unlikely that a common base of understanding will ever develop such that we could ever be considered a united and cohesive group. Similarly, the slave and free early Black Americans experienced this same hurdle until the Civil Rights movement of the mid-twentieth century occurred. It will take a movement just as major that crosses philosophical, economic and cultural lines to bridge the gap that exists between the different groups. In the meantime, we are all lumped into the group largely referred to as African American. This takes none of our differences into account, but does serve socially, politically and economically to brand us as to identification in these United States. Why is this? It is an issue that I will leave to the so-called social, political and economic experts in this country to examine.

For my purposes, I wanted to establish a starting point by giving identity to what is the foundation of Black America today. That is the American of African descent whose history is written and unwritten in the annals of American history. They have been here through the foundation of America. This is important as identities become even more blurred in what is becoming an even more multinational country.

Acknowledgments

I learned a very long time ago as a student and athlete that no one gets ahead in life alone. There are many assists along the way. In my case, I began by researching the works of Dr. Sterling Stuckey, Ph.D of Northwestern University who has written extensively on the culture of African slaves in the United States. I did so in order to test the soundness of my thoughts prior to beginning my writing.

I also wish to acknowledge the assistance of Dr. James P. Pitts, Ph.D of the University of North Carolina, Asheville, for his input and assistance. Beyond that, I owe a great debt of gratitude to a dedicated group of faculty and administrators at a once giant of a high school in north Florida, Carter-Parramore, Quincy, Florida, who instilled in me the foundation and the passion to think and analyze beyond what is apparent or presented and draw my own conclusions. They also recognized and instilled in me the importance of being able to communicate, verbally and written, and would not accept anything less than what they considered to be my best.

About the Author

Woody Campbell was born and grew up on a tobacco farm in Mount Pleasant, Florida, a small town in Florida's Panhandle about thirty miles west of Tallahassee. He is the son of proud parents who provided him and his siblings (three sisters and a brother) love and guidance without focusing on their condition, but instead instilling in them the need to do better than their parents by using their education and becoming the best they could be.

He graduated valedictorian and star athlete from Carter-Parramore High School, Quincy, Florida. He attended Northwestern University, Evanston, Illinois on an athletic scholarship in football and graduated in four years with a "B" average receiving a B.A. Degree in Arts and Sciences. He, along with Otis Armstrong (Northwestern University) and Cyril Pinder (University of Illinois), pioneered the opening of the state of Florida to big time college football for Black athletes.

At Northwestern, he was a scholar athlete, winning the first two Coca-Cola Golden Helmet Awards as a sophomore and Junior halfback for the Northwestern Wildcats. He was also "first team" All Big Ten Scholar Athlete his junior and senior years. He was an Academic All American Scholar Athlete and was elected to the Northwestern University Junior and Senior Men's Honor Society. As a senior, he was awarded the prestigious Northwestern University Athletic Achievement Award. He also holds the distinction of being the first Black athlete to play and score a touchdown in what is now the vaunted "Swamp" (Florida Field) at the University of Florida.

After leaving college, he was drafted by the Houston Oilers of the National Football League where he was an All Pro Running Back. He was one of only seven professional athletes to serve on active duty in Vietnam. After leaving professional football, he became the first Black sportscaster in the city of Houston. He is a member of the National Football League Players Association (Retired).

He has enjoyed a successful career as a middle manager in corporate America with service of distinction in stops at Control Data, Digital, Compaq, University of Texas M. D. Anderson Cancer Center, and IBM where he was often sought as a mentor and advisor to the many associates he has worked alongside. He is a member of the Houston Chapter of the Project

Management Institute. He is currently seeking to use his acquired experience as a motivation and inspiration to help others as they seek to grow.

Bibliography

Films & Books, Authors, Historical Events

Black Wallstreet, Tulsa (1921)—America's most affluent Black community was destroyed in June by angry mobs of Whites. The mobs burned and looted, killing hundreds of innocent blacks.

Medgar Evers (1925-1963)—Black civil rights activist from Mississippi. He was assassinated in June, while working to advance the cause of Blacks in Mississippi.

Marcus Garvey (1887-1940)—Garvey was born in Jamaica. He was a Black Nationalist leader whose Negro Improvement Association (NIA) was the most prominent Black power organization of the 1920's.

D. W. Griffith (1875-1948)—American film director best known as director of controversial film *The Birth of a Nation* (1914).

Alex Haley (1921-1992)—Author of monumental best seller *Roots* and winner of Pulitzer Prize for non-fiction. *Roots* became a TV mini-series. Haley traces his family history through the drama of nineteenth-century slave Kunta Kinte.

Rosewood—A film by the same name, made by John Singleton (1997)—Depicted the massacre of the predominately black town of Rosewood, Florida by angry Whites alleging an attack on a White woman.

Sterling Stuckey—Noted author on Black slave life and culture. One of his works, *Slave Culture: Nationalist Theory and the Foundations of Black American* (paperback), received the following review:

> *Stuckey's stimulating work clearly suggests that until Afro Americans can resolve not only the problems of economic and political empowerment but also the problem of cultural self-definition—especially as regards their Africaness—the travail of Black liberation will not come to an end.*
>
> *—The Nation*

The 54th Massachusetts—All Black volunteer regiment from Massachusetts who fought in the Civil War and became the subject of the movie *Glory*.

Booker T. Washington (April 5, 1856 to November 14, 1915)— American (Black) political leader, educator and author; he was one of the dominant figures in Black American history in the United States.

Political Acts, Amendments

Civil Rights Act of 1964 and Voting Rights Act of 1965— Guaranteed basic civil rights for all Americans, regardless of race.

Three-Fifths Compromise—A compromise between Northern and Southern States during the 1787 United States constitutional convention that declared a slave would be counted as three-fifths of a person for purposes of representation.

Named Historical References

Crispus Attucks (1723-1770)—A Black man who became the first casualty of the American Revolution when he was shot and killed in the Boston Massacre.

Sojurner Truth (Isabella Baumfree), (1797-1883)—American abolitionist born into slavery, who was also an advocate of women's rights.

Harry Belafonte (born March 1, 1927)—Black Harlem-born actor/singer, activist and humanitarian.

Mary McLeod Bethune (1875-1955)—Black educator and activist. Founder of Bethune-Cookman College and the National Council of Negro Women.

Shirley Chisholm (1924-2005)—Politician, educator and author. She was the first Black woman elected to Congress and the first Black American to make a bid for the presidency (1972).

Bessie Coleman (1892-1926)—Black female aviatrix and pioneer who was the first woman to earn an international aviation license.

Ben Hodges—Fast-talking, well-known gambler from Dodge City, Kansas—*The Black West*, by William Loren Katz.

W. E. B. DuBois (1868-1963)—American civil rights activist, Pan-African, socialist, educator, writer, poet and scholar who, at the age of 95, became a naturalized citizen of Ghana.

Mary Fields—A Black gun-totin' female known as "Stagecoach Mary", she was six feet tall, ambitious and as daring as any man. *The Black West* by William Loren Katz.

Althea Gibson (August 25, 1927-September 28, 2003)—First Black female to win tennis Grand Slam tournaments at Wimbledon, The French Open, and the United States Open in the 1950's.

Lena Horne (born 1930)—Internationally known Black female singer/actress.

Sidney Poitier (born February 20, 1927)—Bahamian born Black American award-winning actor, director and activist.

Paul Robeson (April 9, 1898-January 23, 1976)—Multi-lingual Black American actor, athlete, bass-baritone, concert singer, writer and civil rights activist and Levin Peace Prize Laureate.

Bill "Bojangles" Robinson (1878-1949)—Tap dancer, actor who became the first Black American to star in the *Ziegfield Follies* and originated the routine of tapping up and down stairs.

William Robinson (California, Mid 1800's)—Black California Pony Express Rider—*The Black West*, by William Loren Katz.

Dr. Daniel Hale Williams (1856-1931)—Founder of Provident Hospital in Chicago. He was the first doctor to successfully operate on a human heart.

Coleman Young (1918-1927)—Member of the Tuskegee Airmen and the first Black mayor of Detroit who served five terms.

Andrew Young (born March 12, 1932)—American civil rights activist, former mayor of Atlanta and first Black Ambassador to the United Nations.

www.FadeToBlack-TheBook.com